Name _____

D1470360

Fred's Lunch

Fred sits on a lily pad in the pond.

Fred sees a fly.

Gulump! It's gone!

1. **Where** is Fred sitting? _____

2. **What** does Fred catch? _____

3. **Where** does Fred live? _____

Name _____

Pip

Pip is Liam's puppy.

Pip likes to ride.

He rides in a wagon.

He rides on the sidewalk.

1. **Who** owns Pip? _____

2. **What** does Pip like? _____

3. **What** does Pip ride in? _____

4. **Where** does Pip ride? _____

Name _____

Rub-a-Dub

Harry likes bubble baths.
He takes a bath at night.
He sings in the tub.

1. **What** does Harry like?

_____

_____

2. **When** does Harry take a bath?

_____

_____

3. **Where** does Harry sing?

_____

_____

Name

Seeing Stars

Can you see stars in the daytime?

Everyone has seen one.

It is our sun.

Our sun is a star.

1. **What** is our sun?

_____

- - - - - - - - - - - - - - - - - - -

2. **When** do you see it?

_____

- - - - - - - - - - - - - - - - - - -

3. **Who** has seen a star in the daytime?

_____

- - - - - - - - - - - - - - - - - - -

Name _____

Bun Has Fun

Bun is playing a _____ .

What?

She is hiding from her _____ .

Who?

She is hiding _____ .

Where?

> **Spelling Help**
> in a box
> game
> sister

Name _____

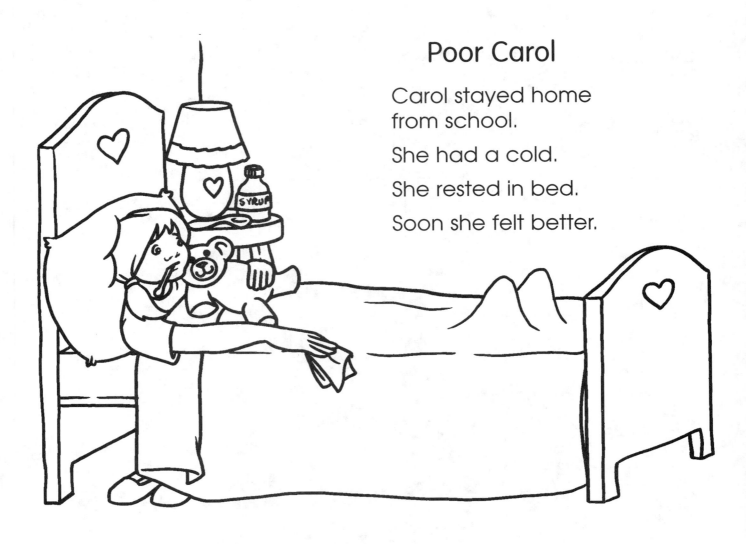

Poor Carol

Carol stayed home from school.

She had a cold.

She rested in bed.

Soon she felt better.

1. **Why** did Carol stay home from school?

_____

_____

2. **What** did Carol do?

_____

_____

3. **When** did she feel better?

_____

_____

Name _____

Sal

Sal is a farm horse.

She has a funny hat.

She wears it on sunny days.

1. **Where** does Sal live?

   _____

   _____

2. **What** does she have?

   _____

   _____

3. **When** does she wear it?

   _____

   _____

Name _____

A Pretty Picture

Tasha is happy.

She painted a pretty picture.

She gave it to Mom as a birthday present.

1. **Who** is happy?

_____

_____

2. **What** did Tasha paint?

_____

_____

3. **Why** did she give it to Mom?

_____

_____

Name _____

Chipper

It is fall.

Chipper Chipmunk gathers acorns to hide for the coming winter.

He carries them home in his cheeks.

1. **What** season is it?

   O winter   O fall   O spring

2. **Why** is Chipper gathering acorns?

   O to save for later   O to eat now   O just for fun

3. **Where** does Chipper carry the acorns?

   O in his cheeks   O in his home   O in a tree

4. **When** will he eat the acorns?

   O in the summer   O in the fall   O in the winter

Name

Whoops!

A button came off my jacket.

Grandma went right to the closet.

She got her sewing basket.

She sat in her chair and fixed the button.

1. **What** needed to be fixed?

   ○ a button   ○ a basket   ○ a closet

2. **Where** was Grandma's sewing basket?

   ○ in the jacket   ○ in the closet   ○ under her chair

3. **Where** did Grandma sew?

   ○ in the closet   ○ at the table   ○ in her chair

4. **When** did Grandma fix the problem?

   ○ right away   ○ never   ○ before it happened

Name _____

A Lizard

This lizard lives in the desert. It is the color of sand. Its color helps it hide from enemies. It can also run fast if it spots danger.

1. **Where** does this lizard live?

   _____

   _____

2. **What** color is the lizard?

   _____

   _____

3. **What** does the lizard hide from?

   _____

   _____

4. **When** does the lizard run fast?

   _____

   _____

Name _____

Bingo

Bingo is Davy's cat.

She sits in the window.

She watches birds in the tree outside.

Sometimes she makes noises at them.

1. **Where** does Bingo sit?

_____

3. **Who** owns Bingo?

_____

2. **What** does she watch?

_____

4. **When** does she make noises at the birds?

_____

Name _____

The Toy

Joann saved money for a toy.

When she got it home, it didn't work.

She took it back to the store.

1. **Who** paid for the toy? _____

2. **Where** did Joann get money for the toy? _____

3. **Where** did she buy the toy? _____

4. **Why** did she take it back? _____

Name _____

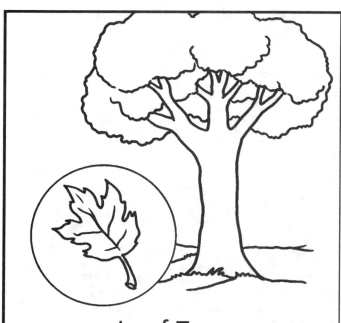

Leaf Tree

This tree changes each season. It has leaves in the summer, loses them in fall, and grows new ones in spring.

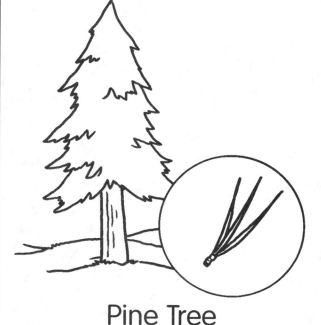

Pine Tree

This tree has needles. It keeps its needles all year long. It also has pine cones, where new tree seeds grow.

1. **When** do leaf trees lose their leaves?

2. **What** kind of tree has needles?

3. **Where** are pine tree seeds found?

4. **What** kind of tree changes with the seasons?

Name _____

A Winter's Nap

Use the 5 W's to make up a story about the picture. Fill in the answers below. Then be ready to tell your story.

Words You Might Like to Use

Bear   winter   sleep   wake
food   spring   cave   hungry
grumpy   yawn   stretch   look

1. **Who**?

_____
- -
_____

2. **What**?

_____
- -
_____

3. **Where**?

_____
- -
_____

4. **When**?

_____
- -
_____

5. **Why**?

_____
- -
_____

Name _____

Guide Dogs

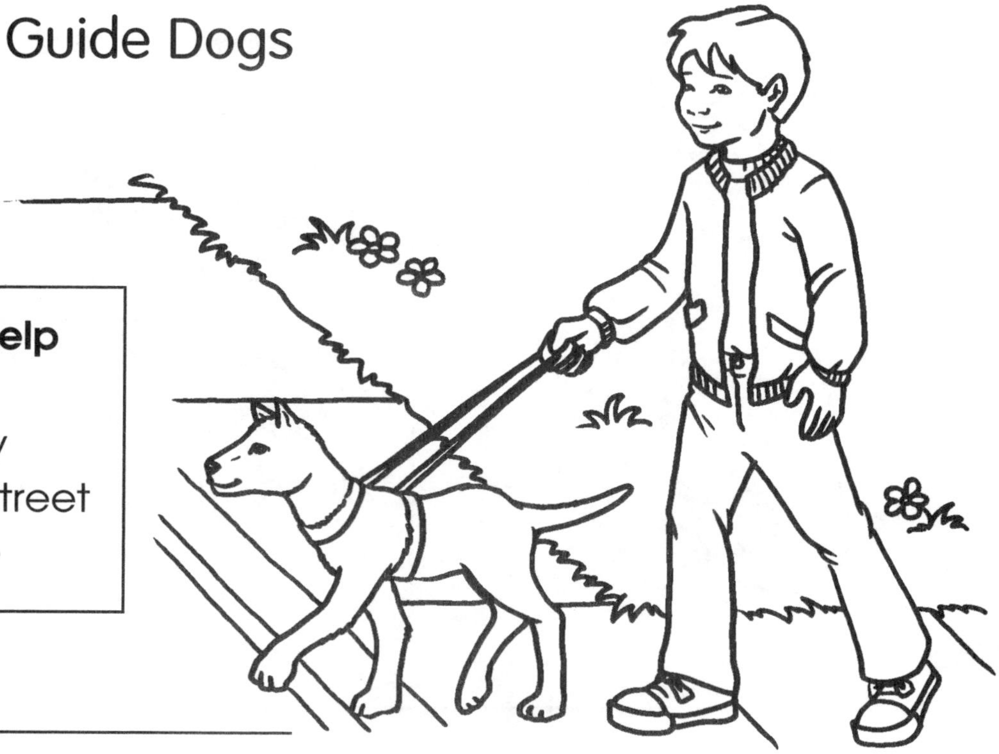

Spelling Help
dogs
disobey
across the street
people

Some _____ are very special. They are trained
What?

to help _____ who cannot see.
Who?

Guide dogs are trained to watch for dangers and guide

people safely _____ .
Where?

A guide dog will even _____ an order
What?

if it puts its master in danger.

Name _____

It's Time

Dad said when Tom was seven he could have a pet.

Tom just turned seven.

Next week, Aunt Susan will take Tom to the pet store where she works to pick out a pet.

1. **Who** wants a pet?

   _____
   _____

2. **Where** does Aunt Susan work?

   _____
   _____

3. **When** will Aunt Susan take Tom to the pet store?

   _____
   _____

4. **Why** is Tom allowed to have a pet now?

   _____
   _____

5. **What** will Tom and Aunt Susan do at the pet store?

   _____
   _____

Name _____

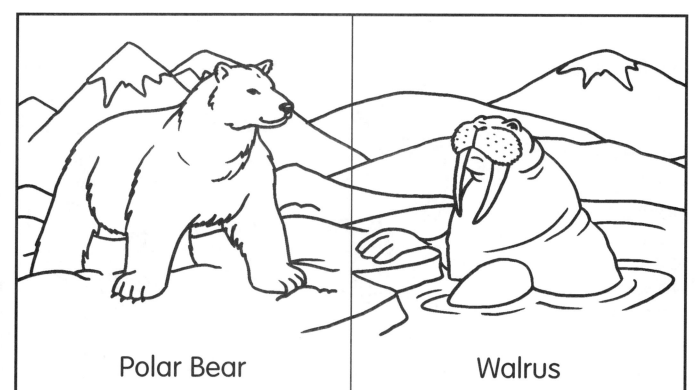

Polar Bear

The polar bear lives in very cold places. It has a thick coat of white fur to keep it warm. Polar bears swim well but live mostly on the ice where they hunt seals.

Walrus

The walrus also lives in these cold places. It has a thick layer of fat to keep it warm. Walruses spend much of their time in the water, gathering clams and shellfish.

1. **Where** do these animals live?

   _____

   _____

2. **Why** does a walrus have so much fat?

   _____

   _____

3. **Where** does a walrus find food?

   _____

   _____

4. **What** would be a meal for a polar bear?

   _____

   _____

Name _____

Shopping

Mark was growing out of his clothes.

On Saturday, Dad took Mark shopping.

Grandma said she would stay home with little Nora so they could finish their shopping faster.

1. **Where** did Dad and Mark go?

   O Grandma's   O shopping   O school

2. **When** did Dad and Mark go?

   O Sunday   O Saturday   O Friday

3. **Who** were they shopping for?

   O Dad   O Nora   O Mark

4. **Why** did Mark need new clothes?

   O He had grown.   O His old ones were torn.

5. **Who** is the youngest person in the story?

   O Mark   O Grandma   O Nora

Name _____

Brrrrrring!

The phone rang.

Joey answered it.

It was Jean calling for his big sister, Judy.

He went to Judy's room to tell her.

Judy came down to the kitchen right away.

1. **Who** is Judy?

_____

- - - - - - - - - - - - - - - - - - - -

_____

2. **Where** was Judy when the phone rang?

_____

- - - - - - - - - - - - - - - - - - - -

_____

3. **Why** did Joey go to Judy's room?

_____

- - - - - - - - - - - - - - - - - - - -

_____

4. **Where** in the house is the phone?

_____

- - - - - - - - - - - - - - - - - - - -

_____

Name _____

A Little Nap

The family left just after lunch. Little Mouse had a big meal of the bread crumbs they dropped under the picnic table. He yawned and soon was fast asleep.

1. **Who** fell asleep?

   _____
   _____
   _____

2. **When** did the family leave?

   _____
   _____
   _____

3. **What** did Little Mouse find to eat?

   _____
   _____

3. **Where** did Little Mouse find his lunch?

   _____
   _____
   _____

Name _____

Thank You

Jay got a package.

It was books about his favorite thing—dinosaurs.

Right away, Jay wrote a thank-you letter to Uncle Jeffrey in Florida.

1. **Who** sent the books? _____

2. **What** does Jay like? _____

3. **Why** did Jay write a letter? _____

4. **When** did he write it? _____

5. **Where** did he send it? _____

Name _____

Measuring Up

Long ago, people measured things with parts of their bodies, such as hands or feet. But, this didn't work well because people's hands and feet are all different sizes.

Now we use standard measurements. A measurement such as a "foot" means the same thing to everyone, no matter what size the person's feet are.

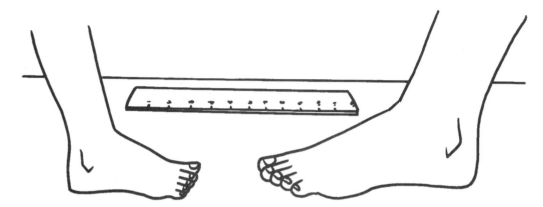

1. **When** did people measure things with parts of their bodies?

   _____

   _____

   _____

2. **Why** didn't this way of measuring work well?

   _____

   _____

   _____

3. **What** does "standard" measurement mean?

   _____

   _____

   _____

   _____

Name _____

Mr. Abel's Hobby

Mr. Abel is building a model railroad just for fun. He works on it every day. When his grandchildren visit, they run right down to the basement to see what he has added.

1. **Why** is Mr. Abel building a model railroad?

   O for his grandchildren   O just for fun   O for work

2. **Where** is Mr. Abel's model railroad?

   O at his grandchildren's house   O in his basement

3. **When** does Mr. Abel work on his hobby?

   O when his grandchildren visit   O every day   O never

Name _____

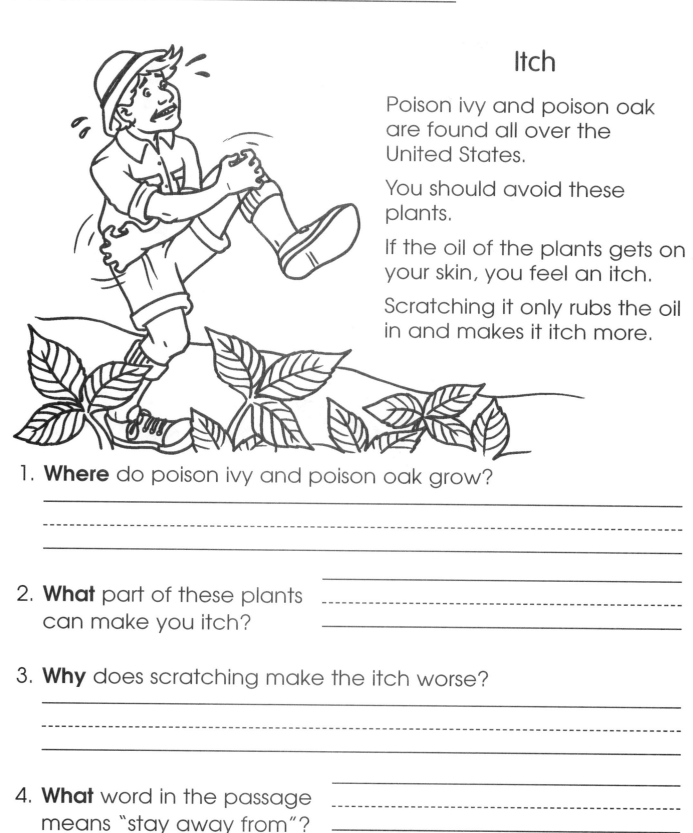

Itch

Poison ivy and poison oak are found all over the United States.

You should avoid these plants.

If the oil of the plants gets on your skin, you feel an itch.

Scratching it only rubs the oil in and makes it itch more.

1. **Where** do poison ivy and poison oak grow?

_____

_____

_____

2. **What** part of these plants can make you itch?

_____

_____

3. **Why** does scratching make the itch worse?

_____

_____

_____

4. **What** word in the passage means "stay away from"?

_____

_____

Name _____

Speckles

Pete has a pet.

It is a bunny.

It lives in the garage.

Pete named the bunny "Speckles" because it has spots.

Pete feeds his bunny lettuce and carrots.

Speckles likes carrots best.

1. **What** kind of pet does Pete have?

2. **Where** does Pete's pet live?

3. **Who** named the pet?

4. **Why** is the pet named "Speckles"?

5. **What** is Speckles' favorite food?

Name _____

Picture Day

Jesse is dressed up.

It is picture day at school.

She will have her picture taken this afternoon.

Jesse likes to get dressed up.

She likes to look nice in her picture.

She will smile for the camera.

1. **Why** is Jesse dressed up?

_____

_____

2. **Where** will she have her picture taken?

_____

_____

3. **When** will the pictures be taken?

_____

_____

4. **Why** does Jesse like to dress up?

_____

_____

Name _____

Work and Play

Dad asked Charlie and Nan to help with the work in the yard.

They are cleaning up the autumn leaves.

After they make a big pile with the rake, they will jump in the leaves just for fun.

Then they will scoop up the pile and put the leaves neatly in bags.

1. **Who** asked the children to help with the work?

   O Charlie   O Nan   O Dad

2. **When** does this story take place?

   O fall   O spring   O summer

3. **Why** will Charlie and Nan jump in the pile of leaves?

   O to make a mess   O to scoop them   O just for fun

4. **Where** are Dad and the children working?

   O in the house   O in the yard   O at school

5. **What** do the children use to make the pile of leaves?

   O a bag   O a scoop   O a rake

Name _____

Joe

Joe is happy. It is his seventh birthday. He is having a party. He invited his best friend, Sam.

Sam

Sam is at Joe's party. He is wearing a party hat. Next month, he will ask Joe to his seventh birthday party.

1. **What** is on Sam's head? _____

_____

2. **Why** is Joe happy? _____

_____

3. **Who** is older, Sam or Joe? _____

_____

4. **When** is Sam's birthday? _____

_____

5. **Where** is Joe's best friend? _____

Name _____

Tall Order

Words You Might Need

tall	reach	word
leaves	able	giraffe
elephant	high	trees

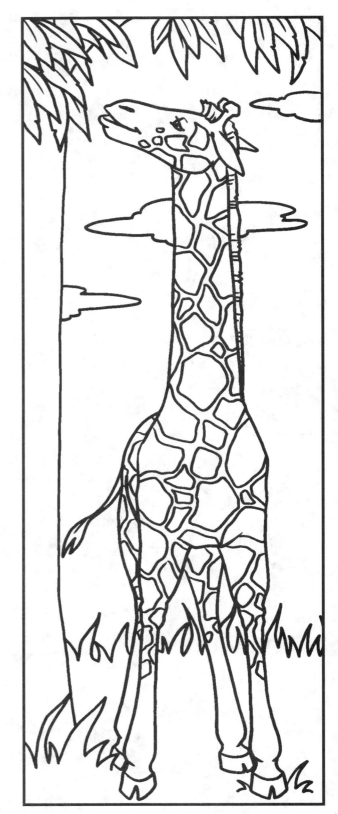

1. **What** animal is in the picture?

_____

_____

2. **What** is it trying to do?

_____

_____

_____

_____

3. **Where** is the food giraffes like found?

_____

_____

4. **Why** do giraffes have long necks?

_____

_____

_____

_____

Name _____

Jumping Fun

Use the 5 W's to make up a story about the picture. Fill in the answers below. Then be ready to tell your story.

Words You Might Like to Use

skip Carla rope playground
friends park good recess
fun contest school time

1. **Who**?

_____

_____

2. **When**?

_____

_____

3. **Where**?

_____

_____

4. **What**?

_____

_____

5. **Why**?

_____

_____

Name _____

Kids-in-the-Kitchen Safety

It can be fun to cook in the _____ .
Where?

But _____ is very important! Never cook or
What?

use a knife without a _____ there.
Who?

Be sure to use a mitt _____
Why?

from getting burned by hot things. To have a safe and fun

time cooking, _____
When?

follow the grown-up's directions

and watch out for dangers.

Spelling Help
always   safety   grown-up
kitchen   to protect you

Name _____

Mr. Porter

Ms. Jones

The Substitute

Ms. Jones, our regular first-grade teacher, was sick.

Mr. Porter came to take her place.

We were a little afraid of him at first because we didn't know him.

But after a while, we found out that he is very nice.

We missed Ms. Jones, but we liked Mr. Porter. We hope he comes back someday.

1. **What** grade does Ms. Jones teach?

2. **Why** was Ms. Jones not at school?

3. **Who** was the substitute for Ms. Jones?

4. **What** did the children find out about Mr. Porter?

5. **When** do the children hope Mr. Porter comes back?

Name _____

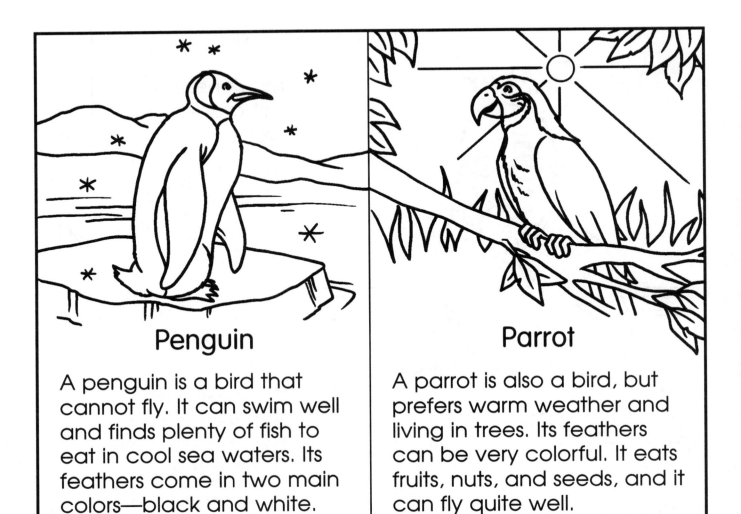

Penguin

A penguin is a bird that cannot fly. It can swim well and finds plenty of fish to eat in cool sea waters. Its feathers come in two main colors—black and white.

Parrot

A parrot is also a bird, but prefers warm weather and living in trees. Its feathers can be very colorful. It eats fruits, nuts, and seeds, and it can fly quite well.

1. **What** weather does a parrot like? _____

2. **What** kind of bird cannot fly? _____

3. **Why** does a penguin need to swim well? _____

Name _____

A Real Koala

Rosie loves koalas. More than anything, she would like to have one for a pet.

Rosie knows that she cannot have a real koala for a pet.

So, for her birthday, she asked for a big stuffed animal.

Can you guess what animal?

1. **What** does Rosie want more than anything?

   O a real koala   O a stuffed koala   O a birthday party

2. **Why** did Rosie ask for a stuffed animal for her birthday?

   O She can't have a pet.   O She can't have a real koala.

3. **Who** do you think Rosie asked for a big stuffed animal?

   O her baby brother   O her parents   O a store

4. **When** will Rosie get a real koala?

   O never   O for her birthday   O soon

5. **What** do you think Rosie will get for her birthday?

   O a real koala   O a stuffed koala   O a pet

Name _____

Who's Nosey?

Bill has a dog. It is a bloodhound with a very sharp sense of smell. That is why she is named "Nosey."

One afternoon, Bill was walking near home with Nosey.

Suddenly, Nosey sniffed and pulled Bill toward the house.

Nosey could tell that dinner was almost ready.

1. **What** word lets you know that Nosey is a girl dog?

   _____

   _____

2. **When** does this story take place?

   _____

   _____

3. **Where** were Bill and Nosey walking?

   _____

   _____

4. **Why** is Bill's dog named "Nosey"?

   _____

   _____

Name _____

Bake Sale

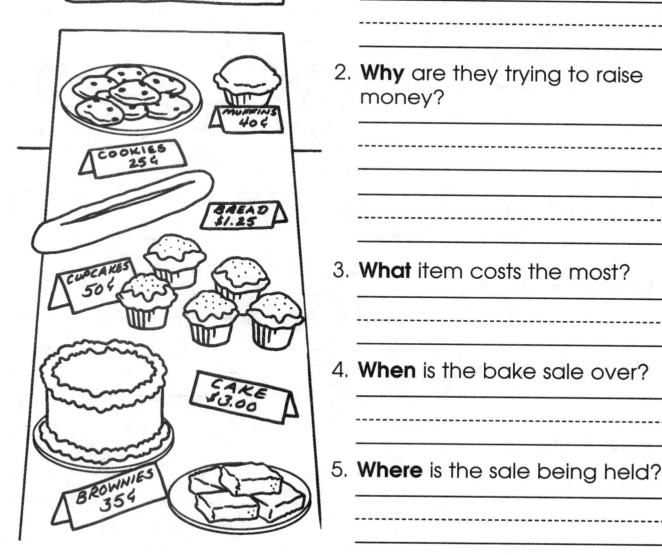

Words You Might Need
computers 4:00 lunchroom
school buy cake 3:00
teachers books children

1. **Who** is holding the bake sale?

    _____

    ----

2. **Why** are they trying to raise money?

    _____

    _____

3. **What** item costs the most?

    _____

    _____

4. **When** is the bake sale over?

    _____

    _____

5. **Where** is the sale being held?

    _____

Name _____

Two Points

On Saturdays, Sherry and her dad spend the afternoon together.

One thing they like to do is shoot baskets in the driveway.

They play just for fun, but they still keep score. The first one to get 50 points wins.

Later, Dad buys them each an ice cream cone.

They both enjoy their time together.

1. **When** do Sherry and her dad spend the afternoon together? _____

2. **What** kind of ball do they play with? _____

3. **Where** do they play? _____

4. **Why** do they play? _____

5. **Who** buys the ice cream? _____

Name _____

Up and Away

Dana was excited.

It was the day the city was launching a hot-air balloon to celebrate its 100-year anniversary.

Everyone gathered in the field to watch.

The fire was lit and the balloon inflated.

The ropes were untied and the balloon went up and away.

1. **Why** was Dana excited?

_____

_____

2. **Who** was celebrating an anniversary?

_____

_____

3. **What** does "inflated" mean in the story?

_____

_____

4. **Where** was the balloon launched?

_____

_____

Name _____

Little Butterfly

Mom told Su-Lin that Grandma is not feeling well.

Su-Lin decided to make a get-well card for her.

She decorated the front of the card with butterflies because Grandma calls Su-Lin "Little Butterfly."

Su-Lin hopes the card will cheer up Grandma and help her get well soon.

1. **Who** is "Little Butterfly"?

   O Su-Lin   O Grandma   O Su-Lin's mom

2. **What** did Su-Lin decide to do?

   O catch butterflies   O buy a card   O make a card

3. **Why** did Su-Lin make a card for Grandma?

   O Su-Lin was sick.   O Grandma does not feel well.
   O Grandma likes butterflies.

4. **Where** on the card did Su-Lin put butterflies?

   O on the front   O on the inside   O all over it

5. **When** does Su-Lin hope Grandma will feel better?

   O Friday   O soon   O tomorrow

Name _____

What an Invention!

Chester Greenwood grew up in Maine where winters are very cold. To keep his ears warm, he invented earmuffs. He got a patent for his invention in 1877. Have you ever used Chester's invention?

1. **What** invention is the passage about? _____

2. **Who** invented them?

_____

3. **When** did he get a patent for his invention?

_____

4. **Where** did he live?

_____

5. **Why** did he need this invention there?

_____

Name _____

Anna

Anna is the oldest of three children. She is in sixth grade and likes to read.

Carl

Carl is in fourth grade. He won a science prize last year in school.

Dan

Dan is seven. He loves animals and playing outside with their dog.

1. **Who** is the youngest child?
_____
_____

2. **Where** does Dan like to play?
_____
_____

3. **When** did Carl win a prize?
_____
_____

4. **What** does Anna like to do?
_____
_____

5. **Who** is the middle child?
_____
_____

6. **What** pet do they have?
_____
_____

Name _____

Imagine That

A dog named "Nip"
Took a summer trip
To meet his pen pal, Matt.

He boarded a plane
And went to Spain
Where his old friend sat.

The look in Nip's eyes—
What a surprise!
He didn't know Matt...is a cat!

1. **Who** boarded a plane? _____

2. **Where** does Matt live? _____

3. **What** was the surprise? _____

4. **When** did Nip take his trip? _____

5. **Why** is the poem titled "Imagine That"? _____

_____

Name _____

I Like Cereal

I like cereal—corn cereal, rice cereal, oat cereal, and wheat cereal. I like hot cereal and cold cereal. But, I especially like cold cereal because it is crunchy. I eat cereal in the morning and at night. I would eat it for dinner if Mom let me. I like cereal so much that Mom sometimes calls me "The Amazing Cereal Man"!

1. **What** four kinds of cereal grains does the writer like?

_____

_____

_____

_____

2. **When** is the writer NOT allowed to eat cereal?

_____

_____

3. **Who** is "The Amazing Cereal Man"?

_____

_____

4. **Why** does the writer like cold cereal better than hot?

_____

_____

_____

_____

Name _____

Dino-Might

Use the 5 W's to make up a story about the picture. Fill in the answers below. Then be ready to tell your story.

Words You Might Like to Use

Luis   fierce   today   long ago
dinosaur   extinct   roamed
mighty   movie   Tyrannosaurus

1. **Who**?

_____

_____

2. **When**?

_____

_____

3. **Where**?

_____

_____

4. **What**?

_____

_____

5. **Why**?

_____

_____

Name _____

Words You Might Need

picture
Friday
him
zoo
today
to buy candy
wife
as a reward
sidewalk
me

Lost and Found

Last _____ on my way home from school,
When?

I saw a wallet on the _____ .
Where?

Inside was a man's _____ and address.
What?

He lived nearby, so I took the wallet to _____ .
Who?

He gave me a dollar _____ .
Why?

Name _____

The Unicorn

This animal looks something like a horse but has one long spiral horn on its forehead.

Unicorns often appear in old Roman and Greek stories called myths. These stories tell of many fanciful creatures and events.

Have you ever seen a unicorn? Of course you haven't because unicorns are only imaginary.

1. **Why** has no one ever seen a unicorn?

   _____
   _____
   _____

2. **What** two words in the passage mean "make-believe"?

   _____
   _____
   _____

3. **Where** is a unicorn's horn?

   _____
   _____
   _____

4. **Who** told of unicorns in ancient stories?

   _____
   _____
   _____

Name _____

Round and Round

Have you ever ridden on a Ferris wheel?

Today, most Ferris wheels are about 45 feet high and carry about 32 people. They are used at fairs and ridden just for fun.

More than 100 years ago, G.W. Ferris invented this wheel. He built a huge wheel that was 250 feet across and could carry more than 2,000 people. It was first used in Chicago in 1893.

1. **Who** invented the huge wheel? _____

2. **Where** was the huge wheel first used? _____

3. **When** was the huge wheel first used? _____

4. **Why** are Ferris wheels ridden? _____

5. **What** shape is a Ferris wheel? _____

Name _____

Plants We Eat

We eat many kinds of plants and different parts of plants.

Some, like apples and strawberries, are the fruits of plants.

Others, like lettuce, are the plant's leaves. Potatoes are the roots of a plant, and peas are the seeds.

Everyone should eat fruits and vegetables every day. They are packed with vitamins and minerals that we need.

1. **What** are fruits and vegetables?

   O parts of roots   O parts of plants   O vitamins

2. **Where** do potatoes grow?

   O underground   O on leaves   O on trees

3. **Who** should eat fruits and vegetables?

   O plants   O everyone   O every day

4. **Why** should we eat fruits and vegetables?

   O They are good for us.   O They taste good.   O They grow.

5. **When** should we eat fruits and vegetables?

   O never   O everyone   O every day

Name _____

The Zebra King

Everyone knew Lion was king of Africa.

One day while Lion was out hunting, Zebra pretended to be king.

He put on an animal hide the golden color of Lion's. He made a crown of leaves and a staff from a tree branch. He stood high on a rock and tried to roar.

Then suddenly Zebra quickly ran off and hid in the tall grasses, leaving his costume behind. The real king was back.

1. **Where** do Lion and Zebra live? _____

2. **Who** did Zebra pretend to be? _____

3. **What** color is a lion's hide? _____

4. **Why** did Zebra run off so suddenly and quickly? _____

Name _____

Problem Solved

Margaret was trying hard at school, but was having trouble.

Then the teacher noticed that Margaret squinted when she was reading.

The teacher sent a note home with Margaret. The next day, Grandma took Margaret to the eye doctor.

On Monday, Margaret came to school in new glasses. Soon she was no longer having trouble with schoolwork.

1. **Why** was Margaret having trouble with schoolwork?

_____

_____

2. **Who** figured out what the problem was?

_____

_____

3. **What** was in the note that the teacher sent home?

_____

_____

4. **When** did Grandma take Margaret to the eye doctor?

_____

_____

Name _____

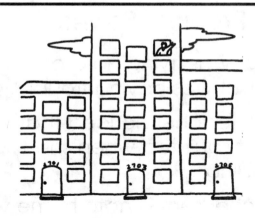

Jake's Apartment

Jake lives in an apartment. There are many families in his building, so he has many neighbors close by. Jake likes living on the eighth floor because he can see much of the city from his window.

Ellie's House

Ellie lives in a house with her mother and her aunt. The house is two stories tall and not attached to another building. From her window, she can see her friend's house next door.

1. **Who** lives on the eighth floor? _____

2. **Where** is Jake's apartment? _____

3. **Where** is Ellie's friend's house? _____

4. **Who** does Ellie live with? _____

5. **What** do both buildings have? _____

Name _____

Time Machine

Even though I know there is no such thing, just for fun I sometimes imagine I could travel in a time machine.

I would go back to the time when there were knights in shining armor. I would ride a great white horse and look for dragons to fight.

I would call myself "Sir Ride-a-lot" and live in a grand castle.

1. **What** would the writer like to use to travel?

    ○ an airplane   ○ a time machine   ○ a horse

2. **Who** is "Sir Ride-a-lot"?

    ○ an imaginary character   ○ a horse   ○ a dragon

3. **Where** would "Sir Ride-a-lot" live?

    ○ in a time machine   ○ in a castle   ○ in a cave

4. **When** does this story take place?

    ○ in the future   ○ in the present   ○ in the past

5. **Why** does the writer imagine going back in time?

    ○ because he does not like the present   ○ just for fun

Name _____

Josie's Surprise

You are invited to join the fun at the King Skating Rink on Saturday, January 24, to surprise Josie on her birthday. The party will begin at 2:00 P.M. You do not need to bring skates or any money. Everything will be taken care of. Just be sure someone is there to pick you up at 4:30 P.M.

1. **Who** is the party for?

   _____

   _____

2. **When** is the party?

   _____

   _____

   _____

3. **Why** is the party being held?

   _____

   _____

4. **When** will the party be over?

   _____

   _____

5. **Where** is the party being held?

   _____

   _____

   _____

I hope you can make it. Josie would love to have you there. Please call Mrs. Hernandez (Josie's mom) at 555-1698 to say if you'll be joining us.

6. **Who** is giving the party?

   _____

   _____

Name _____

Ladybugs

You probably know the ladybird beetle as the ladybug. There are about 150 kinds of these small round beetles.

They can be harmful to some crops. But they help fruit growers control other insects. In the early 1900s, plant lice nearly destroyed the fruit crop in California. Ladybugs were brought in to save the crop.

Today, you can buy ladybugs to add to your garden at home.

1. **What** is the ladybird beetle also called?

2. **Who** finds them especially helpful to have around?

3. **Where** was there a great problem with plant lice?

4. **When** did this big problem happen?

5. **Why** were ladybugs brought into the fruit orchards?

Name _____

Chocolate

Chocolate is made from the seeds of the cacao tree. These trees grow in hot, wet climates.

Long ago, a Spanish explorer named Cortés found people in Mexico who made a drink they called chocolate. It was made with peppery spice. The men tried it, but they only liked it when they replaced the spice with sugar. About 1600, chocolate made its way to Europe and became very popular.

1. **What** did the Mexicans call their peppery drink?

   _____

   _____

2. **Who** found people in Mexico drinking chocolate?

   _____

   _____

3. **Where** do cacao trees grow?

   _____

   _____

4. **When** did chocolate make its way to Europe?

   _____

   _____

5. **Why** did the Europeans replace the spices with sugar?

   _____

   _____

Name _____

Snail

This garden snail likes to dine on green plants. If disturbed, it hides its whole body in its hard protective shell. The shell is made of one piece that coils in a spiral shape.

Scallop

The sea scallop also has a protective shell, but it has two parts that it can open and close. The water flows through, and it catches tiny creatures in its shell for its meal.

1. **When** does a snail hide?

_____

_____

2. **What** has a shell with 2 parts?

_____

_____

3. **Where** does the scallop live?

_____

_____

4. **What** shape is the snail's shell?

_____

_____

5. **Why** do both the snail and the scallop have shells?

_____

_____

_____

Name _____

Little Miss Muffet

Little Miss Muffet sat _____ ,
Where?

Eating her _____ .
What?

Along came _____
Who?

And sat down _____ ,
Where?

Which frightened _____ away.
Who?

Spelling Help
curds and whey
a spider
Miss Muffet
on a tuffet
beside her

Name _____

Flying Fish?

I spent last summer with my grandpa in California. One day we went out in a big boat. Captain Louis told us to be on the lookout for flying fish.

At first I thought he was just kidding—fish can't fly. But then I saw one! Grandpa explained that the fish don't really fly like birds, but they leap into the air and spread out their fins. They glide for a moment, then fall back into the sea.

I said, "Grandpa, next you'll be telling me that there are fish that walk." He just smiled and said, "As a matter of fact, Rosa, ..."

1. **Who** told them to watch for flying fish?

2. **Where** did the storyteller see the flying fish?

3. **Why** did she think the captain was kidding?

4. **When** did the storyteller visit her Grandpa?

5. **What** makes you think that Grandpa knows about fish that walk?

Name _____

Roadrunner

This roadrunner lives in the desert. It has a nest of sticks in low bush. It can run very fast. That's how it can catch its favorite meals— lizards and small snakes.

Owl

This owl lives on a farm. It makes a nest of feathers and grass in a hollow tree trunk. It takes to the air at night to hunt for mice and insects.

1. **Where** is the roadrunner nest?

_____

4. **What** uses feathers in its nest?

_____

2. **When** does the owl hunt?

_____

5. **What** does the roadrunner do very fast?

_____

3. **What** does the roadrunner eat?

_____

6. **Where** does the owl live?

_____

Name _____

An Unusual Plant

Ricky went with his aunt to a nursery—a place where plants are grown. There he saw an unusual plant. It looked like it had jaws. He was curious, so he read the information tag. It said the plant was a Venus's flytrap. Inside its "jaws" is a sticky purple substance that attracts flies. When a fly enters, it gets stuck. The trap closes and captures the fly.

Ricky laughed as he thought, "Many insects eat plants, but this plant eats insects!"

1. **What** is the name of a plant that eats insects?

   O Venus's bugtrap   O Purple flytrap   O Venus's flytrap

2. **Who** was Ricky with when he saw the unusual plant?

   O his aunt   O his mom   O his sister

3. **Where** did Ricky see the unusual plant?

   O on Venus   O in the woods   O in a nursery

4. **Why** did Ricky look at the information tag?

   O He was alone.   O He was curious.   O He can't read.

5. **Where** is the sticky purple substance that attracts flies?

   O on the leaves   O on the stem   O inside the "jaws"

Name _____

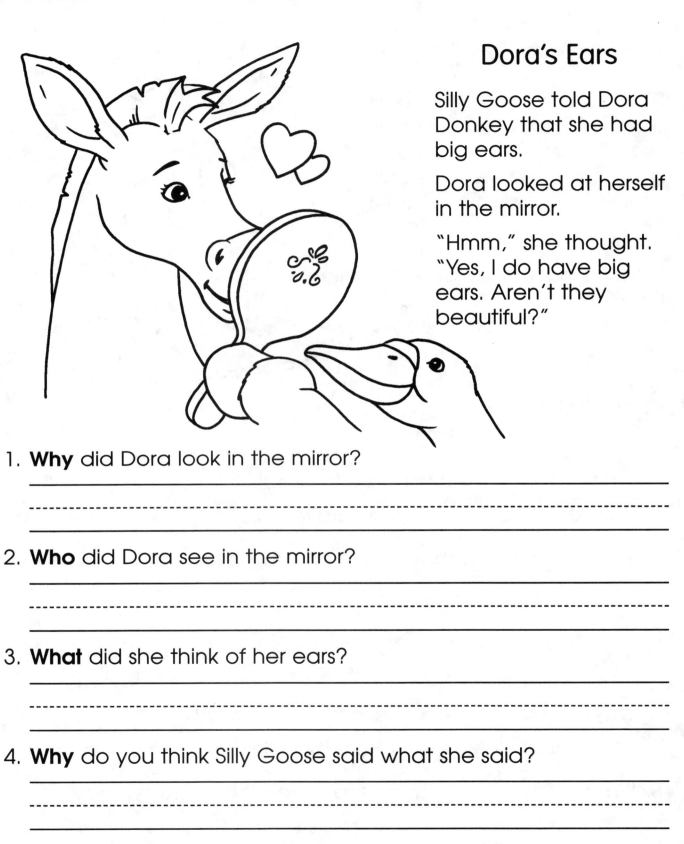

Dora's Ears

Silly Goose told Dora Donkey that she had big ears.

Dora looked at herself in the mirror.

"Hmm," she thought. "Yes, I do have big ears. Aren't they beautiful?"

1. **Why** did Dora look in the mirror?

_____

_____

2. **Who** did Dora see in the mirror?

_____

_____

3. **What** did she think of her ears?

_____

_____

4. **Why** do you think Silly Goose said what she said?

_____

_____

Answer Key for *The 5 W's*

Page 1
1. on a lily pad
2. a fly
3. in the pond

Page 2
1. Liam
2. to ride
3. a wagon
4. on the sidewalk

Page 3
1. bubble baths
2. at night
3. in the tub

Page 4
1. a star
2. in the daytime
3. everyone

Page 5
What?: game
Who?: sister
Where?: in a box

Page 6
1. She had a cold.
2. She rested in bed.
3. Soon she felt better.

Page 7
1. on a farm
2. a funny hat
3. on sunny days

Page 8
1. Tasha
2. a pretty picture
3. for her birthday

Page 9
1. fall
2. to save for later
3. in his cheeks
4. in the winter

Page 10
1. a button
2. in the closet
3. in her chair
4. right away

Page 11
1. in the desert
2. the color of sand
3. enemies
4. if it spots danger

Page 12
1. in the window
2. birds in the tree
3. Davy
4. sometimes

Page 13
1. Joann
2. her savings
3. at the store
4. It didn't work.

Page 14
1. in the fall
2. pine trees
3. on pine cones
4. leaf trees

Page 15
(Answers may vary.)
1. Bear
2. wake, food, grumpy, yawn, stretch, look
3. cave
4. winter, spring
5. sleep, hungry

Page 16
What?: dogs
Who?: people
Where?: across the street
What?: disobey

Page 17
1. Tom
2. at a pet store
3. next week
4. He is seven now.
5. pick out a pet

Page 18
1. in very cold places
2. to keep it warm
3. in the water
4. a seal

Page 19
1. shopping
2. Saturday
3. Mark
4. He had grown.
5. Nora

Page 20
1. Joey's big sister
2. in her room
3. to tell her she had a phone call from Jean
4. in the kitchen

Page 21
1. Little Mouse
2. just after lunch
3. bread crumbs
4. under the picnic table

Page 22
1. Uncle Jeffrey
2. dinosaurs
3. to say thank you for the books
4. right away
5. to Florida (to Uncle Jeffrey)

Page 23
1. long ago
2. People's hands and feet are all different sizes.
3. A "standard" measurement means the same thing to everyone.

Page 24
1. just for fun
2. in his basement
3. every day

Page 25
1. all over the United States
2. the oil
3. It rubs in the oil.
4. avoid

Page 26
1. a bunny
2. in the garage
3. Pete
4. because it has spots
5. carrots

Page 27
1. It is picture day at school.
2. at school
3. this afternoon
4. She likes to look nice in her picture.

Page 28
1. Dad
2. fall
3. just for fun
4. in the yard
5. a rake

Page 29
1. a party hat
2. It is his seventh birthday.
3. Joe
4. next month
5. at Joe's party

Page 30
(Answers may vary.)
1. giraffe
2. reach leaves
3. tall trees
4. so they are able to reach high

Page 31
(Answers may vary.)
1. Carla, friends
2. recess
3. playground, park, school
4. skip, rope, good
5. fun, contest, time

Page 32
Where?: kitchen
What?: safety
Who?: grown-up
Why?: to protect you
When?: always

Page 33
1. first grade
2. She was sick.
3. Mr. Porter
4. He is very nice.
5. someday

Page 34
1. warm weather
2. a penguin
3. to find fish to eat

Page 35
1. a real koala
2. She can't have a real koala.
3. her parents
4. never
5. a stuffed koala

Page 36
1. she
2. in the afternoon
3. near Bill's home
4. It has a very sharp sense of smell.

Page 37
1. teachers
2. to help buy new computers for the school
3. cake
4. 4:00
5. in the lunchroom

Page 38
1. on Saturdays
2. a basketball
3. in the driveway
4. just for fun
5. Dad

Page 39
1. because of the hot-air balloon launch
2. the city
3. filled with air
4. in the field

Page 40
1. Su-Lin
2. make a card
3. to cheer Grandma up
4. on the front
5. soon

Page 41
1. earmuffs
2. Chester Greenwood
3. in 1877
4. in Maine
5. Winters are very cold there.

Page 42
1. Dan
2. outside
3. last year
4. to read
5. Carl
6. a dog

Page 43
1. Nip
2. in Spain
3. Matt is a cat.
4. in the summer
5. A dog has a cat for a pen pal.

Page 44
1. corn, rice, oat, and wheat
2. at dinner
3. the writer
4. because it is crunchy

Page 45
(Answers may vary.)
1. Luis
2. today, long ago
3. movie
4. fierce, dinosaur, roamed, mighty, Tyrannosaurus
5. extinct

Page 46
When?: Friday
Where?: sidewalk
What?: picture
Who?: him
Why?: as a reward

Page 47
1. because unicorns are only imaginary
2. fanciful, imaginary
3. on its forehead
4. Romans and Greeks

Page 48
1. G.W. Ferris
2. Chicago
3. 1893
4. just for fun
5. a circle (round)

Page 49
1. parts of plants
2. underground
3. everyone
4. They are good for us.
5. every day

Page 50
1. in Africa
2. king (Lion, king of Africa)
3. a golden color
4. Lion (the real king) was back.

Page 51
1. She had to squint to read.
2. the teacher
3. (Answers may vary.) I noticed Margaret squinting when she was reading. I think she is having trouble with schoolwork because she cannot see well.
4. the next day

Page 52
1. Jake
2. in the city
3. next door
4. her mother and her aunt
5. (Answers may vary.) windows, more than one story

Page 53
1. a time machine
2. an imaginary character
3. in a castle
4. in the past
5. just for fun

Page 54
1. Josie
2. Saturday, January 24, at 2:00 p.m.
3. to surprise Josie on her birthday
4. 4:30 p.m.
5. at the King Skating Rink
6. Josie's mom (Mrs. Hernandez)

Page 55
1. the ladybug
2. fruit growers
3. in California
4. in the early 1900s
5. to save the crop by controlling the plant lice

Page 56
1. chocolate
2. a Spanish explorer named Cortés
3. in hot, wet climates
4. about 1600
5. They only liked it when they replaced the spice with sugar.

Page 57
1. if disturbed
2. a scallop
3. in the sea
4. a spiral shape
5. for protection

Page 58
1. on a tuffet
2. curds and whey
3. a spider
4. beside her
5. Miss Muffet

Page 59
1. Captain Louis
2. in California
3. Fish can't fly.
4. last summer
5. He smiles and begins to answer.

Page 60
1. in low bush (in the desert)
2. at night
3. lizards and small snakes
4. the owl
5. runs
6. on a farm

Page 61
1. Venus's flytrap
2. his aunt
3. in a nursery
4. He was curious.
5. inside the "jaws"

Page 62
1. to look at her ears
2. herself
3. She thought they were beautiful.
4. (Answers may vary.) to make fun of Dora